The**POWER**of
HOPE

The**POWER**of
HOPE

PATTY MASON

WordCrafts

Contents

Introduction

Dear Friend,

Thank you for making the choice to take this journey with me. Right now your faith may be frail, your hope gone, and your future unclear. Perhaps right now life is hard, even frustrating because you are not experiencing sufficient progress toward a meaningful life fast enough. Most likely the enemy of your soul has been lying to you, and you believe his lies above the truth of God and all the promises He has given you through His Word.

No matter what circumstances come or what life throws at us, we need to learn how to cling to the hope we have in Christ, and believe that God will bring a wonderful result from our trials and pain. The enemy will use hardships and challenges to try to deflate our hope and cause us to become discouraged and depressed. He wants to destroy our hope, because he knows that "Hope deferred will make the heart sick" (see Proverbs 13:12).

Hope brings us peace and gladness of heart because hope is the expectancy of a promising outcome, even when everything seems to be falling apart. In the midst of life's most difficult times, hope is what keeps us going. Hope helps us to hold on to faith and stand firm, even when everything inside of us wants to give up. Hope triumphs on our darkest days! That's the Power of Hope!

It is my constant and hopeful prayer that as you make your way through this workbook and audio CD, that the Lord, by His Spirit, will anoint you with a fresh increase of faith and give you a renewed sense of hope. God has a great plan for your life, so stand firm in the Lord and do not allow fear and unbelief to distract you or persuade you to give up. As you trust in the Lord, He will bring you out of that pit and set your feet upon the solid ground of His love. He will give you a hope and a future filled with joy.

Therefore;

> *"May the God of all hope fill you with all joy and peace as you trust in Him, so that you may overflow with hope by the power of the Holy Spirit."*

Romans 15:13

With Love,

Patty

LESSON 1

The Soil for Hope

"We have this hope as an anchor for the soul, firm and secure."

Hebrews 6:19

Why do you think it is important to have hope? What happens when we feel our hope is gone?

Job 17:15; Proverbs 13:12; Ezekiel 37:11; 1 Thessalonians 4:13

"In the midst of life's trials and trouble we all need hope because without hope we can become emotionally, spiritually, and even physically ill."

God doesn't want us to live without hope.

What happens when our hope is renewed and restored?
Psalm 33:17-22; Isaiah 40:31; 61:1-4, 7

What confident hope is given to those who have faith in God and the Lord Jesus Christ?

Ephesians 2:12-13; Colossians 1:21-23, 27b
Titus 1:1-2; 2:11-14

What warning are we given about where we "put" (NIV) or "fix" (NASB) our hope? What are we *not* to trust in? Who are we to trust in?

1 Timothy 6:17

It is easy to get distracted by the things and pleasures of the world, but our hope is not found in this world. We need to stop finding our confidence, faith, and hope in external things. We find our hope purely through the promises of God and what He has done through the death and resurrection of Jesus Christ. We can live in hope because God has given us His Word and the indwelling Holy Spirit who helps us in our time of need (see John 14:16-18).

Belief in Jesus Christ is the foundation of our relationship with God, and holding onto the hope we profess in Christ and His eternal promises will help us to hold on to faith, and overcome our doubts and the lies of the enemy (the devil) when we are tested by the trials of life.

"No matter where you are right now in life, when you rely on this expectant hope and the promises God has given you through His Word, you will find power and the strength to go on. I want to encourage you in the hope you have in Christ. Whatever you are facing, whatever the trials or times of trouble, it is never hopeless."

Suffering is the soil that gives hope a chance to grow; but, in order for hope to develop, we must allow the right kind of seeds to be planted in our hearts and minds.

What type of seeds should we allow to take root in our hearts and minds? What is the good seed?

Matthew 13:3-8; 18-23; 24

What happens when we don't allow good seed to take root in our hearts and minds?

Matthew 13:3-8; 18-23; 24

What kind of seeds does the enemy *sow* (NIV) or *plant* (NLT)?

Matthew 13:25

What does the Bible say about planting and reaping?
Proverbs 11:18; Galatians 6:7

Like dandelions blowing seeds in the wind, the words we receive—good or bad—will either increase and build up our hope or diminish and even squash our hope. God's word, the words we allow others to speak over us (even the words we speak to ourselves), and the lies of the enemy, are seeds that can take root in our hearts and minds. And these seeds will either produce a rich crop of peace and joy, or they will turn our souls into an emotional weedy mess.

What does the Word of God say about the power of words?

Proverbs 10:11, 19-21, 31-32; Proverbs 18:21; James 3:6-10

What did Jesus say about the words that we speak?
Matthew 12:33-37; 15:11; Luke 6:45

Words can bring death and they can bring life. Positive, uplifting words are a fountain of life that brings hope, peace, and joy to the soul and those around him. Negative, discouraging words drain the life right out of a person, and can spread all kinds of evil. And, according to Jesus, the type of words we speak, whether positive or negative, come from the heart.

Consider the following four sets of verses. What are the types of thoughts and words we can "plant" in the soil of our hearts and minds that will reap hope?

1) Matthew 9:28-30a; 17:20; Luke 7:50; 17:6

2) Psalms 34:1; 35:28; 51:15; 1 Peter 4:11

3) Ezra 3:11; Psalms 95:2; 100:4

4) Ephesians 4:32; Colossians 3:13

Forgiveness, faith, and praise, especially praise mixed with thanksgiving, are powerful words of righteousness that will reap a harvest of hope in any garden of life—whether in a season of blessing or in a season of difficulty.

Now consider the next three sets of verses. What are some of the negative thoughts and words that will choke out hope and produce nothing but weeds?

1) Proverbs 12:25; Matthew 6:25; Luke 8:14; 21:34

2) Luke 24:38; James 1:6, 8

3) Romans 8:15; 2 Timothy 1:7; 1 John 4:18

Fear enslaves our hearts with torment, but there is a kind of fear that will reap hope.

What is the kind of fear that will help us to cling to hope?
Psalm 34:7-9; Proverbs 14:26-27

What does God tell those who struggle with inappropriate fear?
Isaiah 35:3-4; 41:10, 13-14

We have a choice. We can either receive or accept the seeds of righteousness from God's Word with faith, praise and thanksgiving and reap hope. Or we can accept the negative words spoken over us, or choose to believe the lies of the enemy (his seeds of doubt, fear, and worry) that will only choke out any hope that may be developing.

What is growing in your heart and mind? What are the seeds you are receiving? What do you believe?

Examine your thoughts and words. Then you will know if you are growing a garden of worry and despair, or a garden of peace and hope.

If you've been struggling with harmful, negative thoughts and words, it's not too late to stop receiving those negative seeds and start receiving the good seeds of God's Word. No matter what you are growing in your heart and mind, even if it's a garden full of worry, doubt, fear and anxiety, God wants you to take responsibility by admitting that you need help.

Remember, no man can tame the tongue (James 3:8), so you are going to need God's help. And God knows you need His help and wisdom to break the negative cycle. He doesn't expect you to make this change on your own. He wants you to lean on Him and His grace for the strength you need to stop speaking and receiving damaging words, and to start speaking and receiving life giving words.

Make the choice today to stop allowing the seeds of worry, doubt, anxiety and fear to cultivate, and start allowing the seeds of God's Word to grow in your heart and mind. Fill your mouth with praise and thanksgiving, and peace and joy will begin to spring up inside of you.

Pray and ask God to dig up any weedy garden you allowed to grow. Ask Him to remove all the negative plants of wrong and harmful thoughts and attitudes (see Matthew 15:13).

Then ask Him to help you plant His seeds of faith, forgiveness, thanksgiving and praise in the rich soil of your life, so hope has an opportunity to blossom.

Notes, Thoughts, Prayers

The Soil for Hope

The Power of Hope

The Soil for Hope

The Power of Hope

LESSON 2

Hope in Troubled Times

"Blessed is he whose help is the God of Jacob, whose hope is in the LORD his God...who remains faithful forever. He upholds the cause of the oppressed and gives food to the hungry. The LORD sets prisoners free."

Psalms 146:5-7

With all of the disaster, war, and unrest that is happening in the world today, are you struggling to hold onto hope? Do you get nervous each time you watch the news and hear about another event?

How does Jesus tell us to handle hard times? What are we to do? What should we not do?

Matthew 6:34; John 16:33

"Many people today are living without hope. When we focus on the things that are happening in the world around us, it is easy for us to worry and get upset. Even many believers are distracted from their pure devotion to Christ because of what we are witnessing in the world, and that distraction leaves an open door for fear to come and settle in our hearts."

18

When we look at what is happening in the world, it is easy to worry and get upset, but Jesus doesn't want us to live worried. He knows times of hardship and trouble will come, but even in the midst of these trials and troubles, He has also made us a promise.

When hard times hit, what does the Bible tell us to do? What is the hope we can cling to in times of trouble?

Psalms 9:9; 46:1; 55:22; 62:5-8; 1 Peter 5:7

In his letter to the church of Corinth, Paul shares how they were suffering all kinds of trials and troubled times. But instead of allowing the hardships to destroy them, where did they put their hope?

2 Corinthians 4:1, 8-9; 6:4-10; 12:10

I really like how the Amplified Bible explains, in far greater detail, the hope they carried:

> *"Therefore, since we do hold and engage in this ministry by the mercy of God [granting us favor, benefits, opportunities, and especially salvation], we do not get discouraged (spiritless and despondent with fear) or become faint with weariness and exhaustion.*
>
> *"We are hedged in (pressed) on every side [troubled and oppressed in every way], but not cramped or cursed, we suffer embarrassments and are perplexed and unable to find a way out, but not driven to despair. We are pursued (persecuted and hard driven), but not deserted [to stand alone]; we are struck down to the ground, but never struck out or destroyed."*

2 Corinthians 4:1, 8-9 (AMP)

> *"So for the sake of Christ, I am well pleased and take pleasure in infirmities, insults, hardships, persecutions, perplexities, and distresses; for when I am weak [in human strength] then I am (truly) strong (able, powerful in divine strength)."*

2 Corinthians 12:10 (AMP)

"Do not allow the trials and troubles of this world to fill your heart with fear and worry. There is hope in these troubled times. Do not allow the media or the circumstances of your life to distract you. Keep your eyes on Jesus and you will find joy."

Paul and his companions were oppressed and crushed in every way and on every side. They suffered all kinds of persecution and hardship; yet, they were not discouraged or hopeless because they held tight to the hope that God was with them and that He was their constant source of support, help, strength and refuge in the midst of everything they were going through.

What assurances are we given for hope? What promises are we given that God will be with us and will help us in our times of trouble?

Psalms 27:5; 34:6, 17-19; 46:1-7; 54:7
2 Corinthians 1:9-10

Why should we not be unsettled by the trials and troubles we face?

Romans 8:35-39; 1 Thessalonians 3:2-4

What purpose is found in our trials? Why should we consider our trials an opportunity for joy?

2 Corinthians 1:3-7; James 1:2-4; 1 Peter 1:6-9

What are some of the things we should do when we are going through something very difficult?

2 Corinthians 10:3-5

2 Corinthians 1:3-4

Galatians 6:9

1 Thessalonians 5:16-18

Hebrews 12:1-3

Proverbs 23:18

"These may be difficult times, but we do not need to worry and be full of fear. In the midst of it all—in the midst of everything we see going on—when we rest in the Almighty, when we keep our focus on Him and His promises, we will find hope in our troubled times."

"Be strong and take heart, all you who hope in the Lord."

Psalm 31:24

Keep your focus on Jesus and remember all He has endured for you, so you do not lose heart. And when your circumstances are overwhelming and harmful thoughts and negative emotions come against you, take them captive by handing everything over to the Savior. Be joyful and positive. Pray about everything. Give thanks to God in every circumstance you go through, remembering that He works all things out for good as He works to conform you into the image of Jesus (see Romans 8:28-29).

Never give up, keep working and doing good, knowing that at the right time you will reap a harvest. Reach out and help others; comfort them with the comfort God has given you. And above all, look to the future with hope.

Notes, Thoughts, Prayers

Hope for Troubled Times

The Power of Hope

LESSON 3

Hope for Depression

"Some sat in darkness and the deepest gloom, prisoners suffering in iron chains." Yet "He brought them from their darkness and the deepest gloom and broke away their chains."

Psalm 107:10, 14

Are you feeling helpless and hopeless? Has depression swallowed your life and you feel like giving up? Do you feel like you are alone in your suffering, and that no one understands or cares?

Depression is a dark and debilitating illness that can happen to anyone. There are many things that can bring on feelings of hopelessness and despair: hard circumstances; loss and grief; trauma and distress; a medical problem, such as a thyroid or hormones that are out of balance; even poor self-image.

"When I was going through depression, I couldn't see any way out of the darkness. Hopelessness consumed me, so I became suicidal. Yet, in the midst of the darkness, at a point when I had given up completely, I found hope."

What does Scripture say about depression, oppression, and despair? Where does depression come from?

Consider the following sets of verses and situations, and then record what brought on the feelings of depression or oppression.

1) What brought Solomon, the richest and wisest king who ever lived, to the depths of despair?

   Ecclesiastes 2:10-11, 17-23; 4:1, 4

   a) According to Psalm 37:3-14; Ecclesiastes 2:24-25, and 5:18-20, how can we defeat feelings of disappointment and discouragement and find satisfaction in all we do?

Pursuing the things of this world over a relationship with God can bring a sense of emptiness and dissatisfaction. When we work to gain wealth and riches; success and power; instead of finding our value and riches in God, we rob ourselves of true treasure and joy in life.

2) According to Psalm 107:10-11 and Proverbs 4:19, what are the effects of sin in our lives?

Sin not only separates us from God's fellowship; but fighting God, or refusing to listen to Him, can bring depression into our lives.

a) However, what happened in Psalm 107:13-14?

b) Record the hope we have in Psalm 107:17-22.

Even in the distress of our rebellion, if we turn back to God and cry out in repentance, He will save us and restore us. The affliction of depression is no match for a redeeming God who hears the cry of a repentant heart.

31

3) According to Isaiah 61:3, what is despair (NIV), heaviness (KJV)?

Depression is a spiritual problem. The enemy of our souls, the devil, knows how to oppress us. He knows how to fill us with hopelessness that will cause us to feel depressed, even when God is at work in our lives. The enemy wants us to live in a pit of defeat and without hope, but God is there to pull us out.

   a) According to 2 Timothy 1:7; Hebrews 13:5b; 1 John 4:4, 5:18, what hope has God given us concerning this spirit of despair?

When we are feeling downcast, oppressed by that spirit of heaviness, we may feel like giving up, but God is always with us. He has not given us a spirit of fear, but His Spirit of love, power, of self-discipline, and a sound mind (KJV). His Spirit is greater than the spirits that try to attack us. In Him we have the victory. We are more than conquers in Christ Jesus (Romans 8:37), and when we know who we are in Christ, secure in His love, the enemy cannot touch us.

4) Consider the story in Matthew 18:21-35. What did Jesus say would happen to the man who refused to forgive?

Consider this parable from an emotional standpoint. When we harbor resentment, anger and unforgiveness toward another, those harmful emotions eat away at our souls, throwing us into an emotional prison of torment that can cause depression. And until we are willing to forgive, we will not be released from that emotional prison of torment.

a) Record the hope we have in Psalm 103:1-5, 8-12 and Psalm 130.

Forgiveness is not for the person who wronged you. Forgiveness is for you. It is God's gift to you. Just as He has forgiven you and removed all your sins as far as the East is to the West, if you forgive those who sin against you, you will find freedom for your soul from emotional torment.

5) In the story of Jonah, Jonah found himself depressed and stuck in the belly of a big fish because of anger and disobedience.

There are many important lessons we can learn from Jonah and the mistakes he made, but the one we need to zero in on is what happens when we become full of anger and resentment. Jonah was angry when God called him to go to Nineveh. He didn't want to speak to the Ninevites because they were his enemy and the enemy of his people, so Jonah ran in the opposite direction.

During his great escape, God sent a furious storm that nearly capsized the boat, so Jonah allowed the men to throw him overboard. At this point, God sent a big fish to swallow Jonah and there he sat for three days and nights—alone and depressed.

   a) But in Jonah 2:1-10, what did Jonah do in his despair?

Once inside that fish, he did some rethinking, and that new thought process brought on a chorus of repentance and a cry for mercy. As a result, God delivered Jonah and gave him a second chance.

   b) After being given a second chance, what did Jonah do (Jonah 3:1-10)?

c) How did Jonah react to the Lord's compassion (Jonah 4:1-11)?

In his compassion, the Lord caused a vine to grow and give Jonah a chance to cool off in the shade and change his attitude, but he refused, so God allowed the vine to die. With no shade for his head, the sun blazed down on Jonah, fueling his anger even more.

I love how God is a God of second chances. We need His mercy every day, but we need to be careful about the things we think about and the words we speak (see Psalm 19:14), because our thoughts and words can actually bring depression into our lives.

When we are angry and upset over things we can't control, our anger can fester in our hearts like the intense heat of the desert sun. Then those thoughts can come out of our mouths like tongues of fire.

d) What does Proverbs 18:21 tell us about our thoughts, attitudes, and words?

e) What does God's Word say about the words we speak? How can our words affect us and others?

Proverbs 12:14, 18; Ecclesiastes 10:12-14a; Ephesians 4:29; James 1:26

f) When our words and attitudes are out of control or have us feeling downcast, what hope can we find in God's words and attitude?

Psalms 12:6; 119:103, 130; Isaiah 55:8-9

Oh, how glad I am that God doesn't think and speak the way we can at times. But there is hope. No matter how many mistakes we've made with our words in the past, God can redeem us and restore us. His words are truth, and by the truth of His words we are set free (see John 8:31-32, 36).

Therefore, let's allow God to change the way we think and speak by renewing our minds with His word and ways (see Romans 12:2 and Psalm 19:7-11).

6) In Psalm 6, why was King David full of anguish and despair? What did David do in his distress?

How many of us fall into the pit of depression because we worry and fret about life—our health, our finances and jobs, our families, our future. We worry ourselves to the point of exhaustion and despair. David wore himself out emotionally by worrying about his life, but he refused to give up hope.

What did Jesus say about worry? Why? What is more important?

Matthew 6:25-34; Luke 12:22-31

What happens to us when we worry?

Proverbs 12:25a; Luke 8:14; 10:38-42; 21:34

What hope can we find for worry and anxiety?
Psalm 23; Philippians 4:6-7; 1 Peter 5:7

"So then, banish anxiety from your heart and cast off the troubles of your body."

Ecclesiastes 11:10

Worry only destroys, distracts, weighs us down, and adds nothing of value to our lives. Hard times and uncontrollable circumstances of loss and tragedy are not the only things that can bring on depression.

According to Scripture, comparison, disappointment, discontentment, discouragement, fear, sin and rebellion, unforgiveness, anger, impure thoughts and motives, worry and anxiety, a bad attitude and negative words can all unleash that spirit of despair and heaviness in our lives.

"I know what happens to a heart that is locked up in the emotional chains of depression, but I also know the freedom that can only come from Jesus. You are not alone. Reach out to Him."

Regardless of how or why we are swallowed up by depression, there is always hope. In the midst of that deep, dark pit—no matter what is happening in life—there is a place where we can turn, cry out for help, mercy, hope, healing, and freedom and experience the deliverance we desperately seek to find.

Consider the following sets of verses for the hope we can have when we are feeling depressed:

1) Where should we look for hope in times of oppression and depression?

   Psalms 9:9; 42:5-6, 11; 103:6; 146:5-7
   Lamentations 3:19-26

2) Who delivers us from despair and turns our darkness into light?

   Psalms 18:28; 40:1-3

3) According to Isaiah 61:1-3, what did Jesus come to do?

4) When we are overwhelmed by life, where can we find refuge and strength? List some of the ways God helps us in our times of struggle.

Psalms 9:9, 18:1-6, 16-19; Psalm 91

5) Who redeems your life from the pit, heals you, loves you, and brings good things into your life?

Psalms 30:1-3; 103:1-5

God and God alone is your Rock, your Refuge, and your strength in times of distress and despair. He is your hope; the one who delivers you from that pit. God may use doctors and medication to help you in your suffering, but only God can heal you from depression and exchange that spirit of despair for His garment of praise. Only God can give you satisfaction in life; comfort and joy in your grief and heartache, and gladness instead of mourning.

If you are sitting in a pit of darkness, in your distress and despair, turn to God and cry out to Him. Write out Psalm 30:8-10 as a personal prayer to God for help in times of depression.

Allow Psalm 30:1-3, 11-12 to be your song of praise to God as you reach out for His help. As you humbly cry out to God, in due time He will lift you up.

Notes, Thoughts, Prayers

The Power of Hope

The Power of Hope

45

LESSON 4

You Are Not Alone

"So do not fear, for I am with you; do not be dismayed, for I am your God. I will strengthen you and help you; I will uphold you with my righteous right hand."

Isaiah 41:10

When we are going through something very difficult, or when we feel the walls of depression close in around us, we can feel alone. Many people, even family and friends may be around us, yet our hearts are lonely and our souls ache within us. We hide the real pain inside, afraid to disclose how we really feel for fear people will not understand or will judge us.

Christians especially hide; convinced it's not okay for a believer to say, "I'm not okay," at least not out loud. Each day we wear a mask and work hard at convincing those around us that we're fine, when deep down inside we are anything but fine. We go to church and pretend—secretly screaming, "Help!" while wearing a smile.

It doesn't always take hard times or depression to get us to feel alone. Sometimes we feel alone when we compare ourselves to others and feel like we don't measure up, or when we move to a new part of the country and don't know anyone yet. We can even feel alone while messaging hundreds of "friends" on social media.

Being too busy can also bring on feelings of loneliness as we immerse ourselves in the overwhelming activities of life.

However, God created us for fellowship. When we don't engage in the companionship we're created for, we feel isolated and alone.

In the beginning, when God created man, what did God say?

Genesis 2:18

For this reason, God gave us each other; and more importantly, He gave us Himself. What are the promises of God?

Deuteronomy 31:6; Joshua 1:5b, 9; John 14:18; Hebrews 13:5b

"Let us find hope and encouragement as we discover that we are never alone in our suffering. Jesus, our Healer, is with us and there is great purpose in all that we go through."

We need to know and understand that God will never leave us nor forsake us, not even in our darkest moments in life. Whatever we go through, He is with us. If we lean on Him, He will strengthen us and encourage us along the way so we don't lose hope.

How do we know that Jesus understands everything we go through, and that He can comfort us and sustain us through the ups and downs of life?

Isaiah 53:2-5; 7-9; Hebrews 2:18; 4:15-16

"Jesus was a man of all sorrows. He knows what you go through, because He is no stranger to suffering. He knows firsthand, every heartache, pain and sorrow you have endured in this life, because He Himself endured these things."

In all that He suffered, how did Jesus endure? Where did Jesus put His focus? Where should we place our focus so we do not grow weary and give up hope?

Isaiah 53:11-12; Hebrews 12:2-3

There may be times when we feel alone, but we are never alone. For this reason, it is vital that we learn to run to Jesus in these moments of loneliness, and allow Him to give us the comfort and encouragement we need.

What does Jesus invite us to do in our weakness?

Isaiah 55:1-3; Matthew 11:28; Mark 6:31

"In knowing Christ and resting in His goodness, our souls can find rest and a peace that transcends all understanding. Not the kind of peace that comes only when life is easy and circumstances are good, but the kind of peace that brings quietness of heart and mind even in the midst of trouble."

Sometimes we feel isolated because we run from people and situations. At times we even run from God, but Jesus invites us into the quiet for a time of solitude so we can find rest for our souls.

There is a big difference between isolation and solitude; and, so often, we tell ourselves we are alone because we confuse the two. As a result, we make the choice to withdraw into ourselves, believing no one cares or understands.

Consider the following three sets of verses. What can we do when we're feeling alone or isolated?

1) Psalms 18:6; 30:2; Ecclesiastes 4:9-10; Jonah 2:2

This first step can be difficult because we will need to admit we have a problem and need help. Pride is what keeps us feeling trapped in isolation when we can't disclose our need for assistance or support. Go to God first (see 1 Kings 22:5b), and ask Him to send you the help you need.

When sharing your needs with others, be specific. People cannot read your mind, so tell them if you need friendship, meals, help with the kids, etc. We often get upset when we think people are not helping us, but if they don't know there is a need, how can they help?

2) Joshua 1:7-8; Psalm 119:11, 105; John 8:31-32; Colossians 3:16a

Secondly, when you are feeling alone, seek strength and encouragement from God's Word. God is your Rock and refuge. He is your comforter—the one who will never leave you or forsake you.

"I believe that it is during the hardest times of our lives that we experience Christ more—more of His comfort, more of His peace, more of His presence."

---

3) Psalms 4:6-7; 16:11; 27:4-5

And finally, seek God's presence in fellowship, there are some needs that can only be met by God.

No matter how dark or bleak a situation may look or feel, you are never alone. There is no trial or temptation that is beyond God and His ability to deliver you (see 1 Corinthians 10:13). Run to Him; allow Him to be your All-in-all. Allow Him to give you the friendship and companionship you were created for through His word, His presence, and the fellowship of others.

Notes, Thoughts, Prayers

You Are Not Alone

The Power of Hope

LESSON 5

Set the Captives Free

*"In my anguish I cried to the LORD, and he answered me
by setting me free."*

Psalm 118:5

**"God did not create you to live as a captive. He created
you for intimacy in relationship with Him. Hold onto the truth
that God loves you, and the hope that He will be faithful."**

Did you know that many people in the Bible also suffered
depression? It's true. Many mighty men and women of God—
who knew God and walked with Him—also knew what it was
like to fall into a pit of despair and hopelessness. The good news
is that God didn't leave them there. By giving them a new
perspective on life, He gave them hope and delivered them.

Consider the following sets of verses and record who
was full of despair and why they felt hopeless.

1) Ruth 1:3-5, 11-21

2) Job 1:13-20; 3:1-3, 11; 17:15

3) Psalms 6:6-7; 42:5-11

4) 1 Kings 19:1-9

In their despair and grief God was with them, and He saw their pain. In the case of Elijah, what did God do to help him in his time of despair? Why did God provide what he did? What did the angel of the LORD instruct Elijah to do? (v. 5)

How did Elijah respond to God's provision? (v. 6)

Sometimes, even when the Lord is answering us, we are so full of despair that we can't let go of the pain, fear, or discouragement long enough to respond to what God is doing. Yet in our despondency, God doesn't give up on us. He continues to reach out and touch us with His care and provision (v. 7).

Why was it important for Elijah to eat the food? (v.7)

If we've been neglecting ourselves, we need to eat physical food, as in Elijah's case, but God's instruction to eat can also be seen as eating spiritual food. Remember what Jesus said:

> *"Man does not live on bread alone, but on every word that comes from the mouth of the Lord."*

Matthew 4:4

Sometimes we feel depressed because we are in a spiritual desert, so it's vital that we also eat spiritually. We need to allow God's Word to give us strength and to renew our minds with truth (see Romans 12:2). We need His truth to break through the lies and redirect our focus—from ourselves and our problems— back on God.

The journey is too much for us—to try and break out of the bonds of depression on our own—but it is not too much for God. He can deliver us in the blink of an eye, but sometimes we will have to walk with Jesus out of that state of mind.

What did Jesus say to those looking for healing?

Matthew 9:6-7; Mark 2:11; John 5:6-9

If we want to get well, we must be willing to get up, take up our mat, and walk with Jesus.

In 1 Kings 19:7-8, after he ate and drank the second time, what did Elijah do?

Elijah returned to God. This is important, because, all too often, depression pulls us away from God.

Once Elijah came to the mountain of God, what question did God ask? (v. 9)

How did Elijah respond to God's question? (v. 10)

When we are downcast, we feel so alone, don't we? It seems that no one understands and no one cares. When I was going through the depression, I felt utterly alone and rejected. The truth is we are not alone—millions are suffering. But depression soaks through flesh and bone; it saturates the mind until it captures the heart and soul. In a hopeless state, our mental image becomes obscure and we fall into unsound judgment. Our brains cannot produce rational thinking, so we convince ourselves of all kinds of things that aren't true which only make us feel worse.

"Sometimes we put ourselves in a pit of despair by the way we think and speak."

God knew Elijah needed a new perspective and needed to be reminded of His mighty power. In I Kings 19:11-12, what did God display? How did God reveal Himself to Elijah?

Many of us think that in order to be set free, God needs to do something drastic. We watch for the ground to shake and look for the instant healing. We want the quick fix, but, so often, God doesn't come to us like that. God wants relationship more than anything. He wants us to get up and walk with Him. As we journey with Him, He mends our broken hearts and delivers us over time. All too often, God will speak to us in that still small voice again and again, but we don't hear it because we're listening for a loud boom of liberation. Stop pursuing the healing and start pursing the Healer—Amen!

Again, when Elijah heard the voice of God, what question did He ask? (v. 13)

How did Elijah respond this time to God's question? (v. 14)

There are times when we can actually keep ourselves living in that pit of despair. How? By doing what Elijah did. When God asked him the same question a second time, *"What are you doing here?"* Elijah gave the exact same answer. Elijah made despair his identity. This is the way it is—nothing has changed—nothing will ever change.

When we start to identify with the pain of despair it becomes a part of us, and we begin to wear it like an overcoat. We tell ourselves over and over: *This is my life; this is who I am.* But that's not true, because God has a plan for our lives.

God wants to set you free. Hear Him asking you;

"Beloved, what are you doing here? Why are you hiding? What are you running from? Come to me. Why are you allowing yourself to remain in this place of hopelessness?"

In 1 Kings 19:15-19a, how did God redirect Elijah's focus? What instruction did God give him?

So Elijah did as the Lord commanded him. He went back through the wilderness to Damascus; and, as a result, he found a new direction for his for life.

Bottom line: There is hope because God has a plan. No matter how deep the pit, God has a plan for your life. If you will just get up and do what He tells you to do, things will change. Get in His Word and eat. Abolish the lies with His truth. Allow His Word to redirect your focus. Remind yourself of the power of God given to you through the Holy Spirit, and all the good things He has done. Don't run from God. Run to God and ask Him to show you the plans and purpose He has for your life. You are not alone. He is with you, and you are in good company.

Many people of the Bible felt the sting of depression, but they didn't stay in that pit. David found the voice of praise. Naomi was blessed by her Kinsman redeemer and given a grandbaby and a new heritage (Ruth 4:13-22). Job was given a double portion of everything he lost, (Job 42:12-16) and Elijah found a new direction and sense of purpose.

If you are lying under that broom tree full of discouragement and pain, God knows where you are, and He will send you what you need to help you sustain the journey to freedom and victory. Take His hand, lean on Him and listen for His still small voice:

> *"Do not fear, for I am with you; do not be dismayed, for I am your God. I will strengthen you and help you; I will uphold you with my righteous right hand."*

Isaiah 43:10

Notes, Thoughts, Prayers

The Power of Hope

The Power of Hope

LESSON 6

Hope in Christ

"No one whose hope is in you will ever be put to shame."

Psalm 25:3

When things go wrong in your life, what is your first thought? As you face troubled times, what do you believe?

What we dwell on and believe makes a difference in whether we live in defeat or victory. In this lesson, we're going to overcome the lies that try to trap us into wrong and harmful attitudes that drag us down and fill us with self-pity and despair.

"When we do not understand or recognize who we are in Christ, we can be swallowed alive by feelings of unworthiness. If we do not recognize the power and authority given to us in Christ, we walk with a lack of faith and a lack of power. If we are to be victorious, then we need to be rooted in who we are "in Christ."

Where does our hope come from?

Psalms 62:5; 65:5

What happens when we put our hope in God and in His Holy Name?

Psalm 52:8-9 (NIV); Isaiah 40:31(NIV); 61:1-4, 7

When we put our hope and trust in God, our strength is renewed. He helps us to flourish, even in times of trouble and hardship. He restores our souls and rebuilds what was destroyed. He exchanges all of our pain and disgrace for gladness and beauty—giving us a double portion of what was lost.

When life is hard and you're feeling overwhelmed and depressed, where do you run?

Exercise: Begin to watch for whom or what you cling to as your hope and support when you are feeling overwhelmed or depressed. Keep a running journal on everything you place your hope in during the day.

Read Psalm 18. What should we put our hope in?

"When we trust who we are in Christ and allow that revelation to go down deep into our souls, we can stand firm against the enemy's schemes. We're not blown by every wind of teaching. We're strong in our faith and unmoved by our circumstances."

Christ alone is our Strength, our Rock and our Refuge throughout life. He is our Savior and constant help in times of trouble. He is the only one who can deliver us from the emotional pit of hopelessness. He is the LORD God Almighty, the only Truth who can break through the lies that try to destroy us. He will be faithful and will save us when we ask for His help. He is a mighty warrior who strengthens us when we are weak and enables us to go the distance—far beyond anything we are capable of doing on our own. He gives us victory and trains us to be overcomers. He avenges us from those who try to harm us and saves us from the traps that are set for us by the enemy of our souls, Satan, who tries to bring discouragement, doubt and fear.

Knowing who we are in Christ will fill us with hope.

What spiritual blessings and promises are we given "in Christ"?

Ephesians 1:3-14

Knowing who we are "in Christ" is absolutely vital for our success in living a life of victory. Therefore, on Him we have set our hope (2 Corinthians 1:10) because Christ in us is our hope of glory (Colossians 1:27).

Knowing who you are "in Christ" and what you have been given "through Christ" brings hope. How do the following verses offer you the hope you have in Christ?

Romans 8:17

Romans 8:37

2 Corinthians 5:17

Ephesians 1:4

Ephesians 2:4 -5

Philippians 4:7

Philippians 4:13

Philippians 4:19

I Peter 2:9

1 John 4:4

"When we are rooted in Christ, immersed in Him, anchored in Him, holding steadfast to the truth we profess, and the authority given to us in Christ—we have power and victory over everything that comes against us. Whether it is trials and troubles, illness, hardship, or loss, whatever comes against us— we are not destroyed."

In Christ you are set free (John 8:36; Galatians 5:1), and an overcomer by the blood of the Lamb and the word of your testimony (Revelation 12:11). In Christ you are free from condemnation and the law of sin and death (Romans 8:1-2). You are hidden with Christ (Colossians 3:3), holy and blameless in His sight (Ephesians 1:4; 1 Peter 1:16). You have been delivered from the power of darkness and transformed into God's kingdom of light (Colossians 1:12-13). You are born of God; the evil one cannot harm you (1 John 5:18). You have direct access to the throne of grace through Jesus Christ (Hebrews 4:14-16). God will be faithful to complete the good work He has begun in you (Philippians 1:6).

Dear One, the next time you find yourself feeling helpless and hopeless, remind yourself of who you are in Christ. Say to yourself: "In Christ, I am accepted. I am God's child (John 1:12), I am justified (Romans 5:1) and one with the Lord in spirit (1 Corinthians 6:17). In Christ, I am secure. I am free from condemnation (Romans 8:1-2), and free from any charges against me (Romans 8:31-34). In Christ, I am established, anointed, and sealed by God (2 Corinthians 1:21-22). I am a citizen of heaven (Philippians 3:20), so I can find grace and mercy in my time of need (Hebrews 4:16). In Christ, I am significant. I am salt and light (Matthew 5:13-14). I am a branch of the true vine (John 15:1, 5). I am chosen and appointed to bear fruit (John 15:16), God's masterpiece created in Christ Jesus to do good works (Ephesians 2:10). I am seated with Christ in the heavenly realm (Ephesians 2:6), and may approach God with freedom and in confidence (Ephesians 3:12)."

No matter how many promises God has made, they are "YES" in Christ.

In Christ you are given strength, power, grace, endurance, mercy and forgiveness. In Christ you are made right with God; no matter who you are or what you've done. In Christ, the old nature is gone and the new has come. In Christ you are made righteous, holy, and blameless; you have nothing to fear and nothing to hide. In Christ you have the power to overcome the forces of darkness and can have victory each and every day. In Christ, you have the power to hope.

Notes, Thoughts, Prayers

The Power of Hope

LESSON 7

Hope for the Future

"Wisdom is sweet to your soul; if you find it, there is a future hope for you, and your hope will not be cut off."

Proverbs 24:14

Some of us do not like to think about the future because of what we see happening in the world today. Fears arise and we worry about what the future will look like or what we will face. Others fear the future, not wanting to think about illness, loss, or death.

But God doesn't want us to worry about the future. God wants us to trust Him for our days here on this earth, whether many or few. And He wants us to hold tightly to all His promises concerning our future in eternity.

Why should we not worry about the future? What has God promised?

Proverbs 23:18; Jeremiah 29:11

"No matter what you go through always remember what the Bible promises: "Hope will not disappoint us, because God has poured out His love into our hearts by the Holy Spirit, whom he has given us. And by this hope we were saved. And this is the hope to which we have been called: Christ in you the hope of glory! We have this hope as an anchor for the soul, firm and secure."

In Ephesians 1:17-20, what three things did Paul pray that the church would grasp and understand?

1)

2)

3)

The New Living Translation really spells it out for us:

"I pray for you constantly, asking God, the glorious Father of our Lord Jesus Christ, to give you spiritual wisdom and understanding, so that you might grow in your knowledge of God (Father, Son, and Holy Spirit).

"I pray that your hearts will be flooded with light so that you can understand the wonderful future he has promised to those he called. I want you to realize what a rich and glorious inheritance he has given to his people.

"I pray that you will begin to understand the incredible greatness of his power for us who believe in him. This is the same mighty power that raised Christ from the dead and seated him in the place of honor at God's right hand in the heavenly realms."

Ephesians 1:17-20 (NLT)

1) When thinking about the future, why is it important to know God and have a revelation of who He is?

Psalms 24:1-2, 7-10; 47:7-8; Lamentations 5:19
Revelation 11:15b; 19:16

The LORD is King over heaven and earth, He reigns forever and ever. God is good, even when life isn't good. God has a plan, and nothing is beyond His reach or understanding. Therefore, we find hope and peace knowing God is in control, and there is nothing He cannot handle or guide us through.

a) Knowing who God is gives us hope for our days here on earth. No matter what we face, what is His guarantee?

Isaiah 41:10; 43:2, 5; Jeremiah 1:8, 19
Romans 8:35; 37-39; Hebrews 13:5b-6

"No matter where you are right now in life, know that you have been given a glorious future filled with hope. And when you rely on this hope and the promises God has given you through His Word, you will find power and the strength to go on."

---

2) What is the wonderful future hope God has promised?

Romans 8:18-30; Colossians 1:3-5, 12-14
1 Peter 1:3-5

a) Why should we not fear death? What do we have to look forward to when our days here on earth are over?

Isaiah 25:8; John 14:1-3; 1 Corinthians 15:54-55
2 Timothy 9-10; Hebrews 2:14-15

The victory is won!

"To live is Christ and to die is gain."

Philippians 1:21

And when we walk through the valley of the shadow of death, the LORD is with us. His rod will protect us and His staff will guide us safely through (see Psalm 23:4).

b) How does the Bible describe our future glory and life? What is the rich and glorious inheritance we look forward to?

Isaiah 60:18; Jeremiah 31:10-14; Zephaniah 3:20 Revelation 19:4-9; 22:1-5

"So there is hope for your future."

Jeremiah 31:17

Right now we may witness wars, decease, grief, and suffering, but there will come a day when everything will be made new and our sorrows, pain and distress will be wiped away and we will rejoice in the presence of the Lord. So cheer up. Don't be afraid! Your days of mourning will come to an end and the sound of weeping and of crying will be heard no more (see Isaiah 65:17-19).

Even though we have the Holy Spirit within us as a foretaste of future glory, we groan to be released from our pain and suffering. Yet we wait anxiously, and with great expectation, for the day when we will receive our full inheritance as sons and daughters. We eagerly look forward to this freedom, for this is the hope we were saved. It's not hope if we can see it, because who hopes for something he already has? But if we hope for what God has promised, we wait for it patiently (see Romans 8:23-25).

3) How does trusting in God's boundless and endless power give you hope for the future, or whatever you may face in the days ahead?

   Exodus 15:6; Psalm 20:6; 147:5; Matthew 19:26

   a) No matter what happens, God holds the future in His hands - our future days and our future glory. He knows the plans He has for us, and nothing will thwart His promises. As we wait in hope for the promises of God and our future with Him, where can we set our expectancy and find the strength to endure?

   Psalm 62:5

   Psalm 119:43

Psalm 119:74

Psalm 130: 3-7

Psalm 147:11

When we put our faith and confidence in the love and power of God and the promises of His Word, His resurrection life comes alive in us and fills us with a renewed sense of hope and joy that will carry us through even the toughest days.

Pen a prayer and ask God to give you a Spirit of wisdom and revelation so that you may know Him better—His goodness, charter, sovereignty, His love and incredible power. Ask Him to flood your heart with light so you may know the hope to which He calls you, so you may find the strength to endure the days ahead and find hope in the future glory to come.

"I am no longer a prisoner of despair! I am a prisoner of hope. I am strong in the Lord and in His mighty power—He is my Rock and my Salvation. My heart is glad and my tongue rejoices! My body will live in hope because He has not abandoned me. He knows my path in life and He will fill me with joy in His presence. So I hold onto courage and the hope in which I boast—for I have the power of HOPE!"

Notes, Thoughts, Prayers

The Power of Hope

The Power of Hope Audio CD

Also available to complement this workbook is a 60-minute Audio CD:

1.) The Power of Hope

2.) Hope for Depression

3.) Hope in Hard Times

4.) You Are Not Alone

5.) The Soil of Hope

6.) Set the Captives Free

7.) Belief that Brings Hope

8.) Holding onto Hope

The CD and workbook can be used separately or together. Great for small group discussion and study.

To order *The Power of Hope Audio CD*, or to find other books and resources to help with depression, go to:

www.libertyinchristministries.com

Extend an Invitation

Patty Mason is on a mission to help others find hope, healing, and freedom from the bonds that keep them trapped in a world of emotional pain. Drawing from her own life experiences and battle with depression, Patty shares her heart with earnest transparency that will leave you in awe of God's grace and goodness. She is a passionate communicator who speaks to the emotional needs of women, inspiring them to let go of a harmful past and find freedom for their souls. Each of her topics is heartfelt, biblically sound, and pertinent to the needs, lives, and struggles of today's women.

To learn more about Patty or to book an event, visit:

www.libertyinchristministries.com

About the Author

Since 1997, Patty Mason has been sharing her story of God's redeeming grace and has appeared on numerous television and radio programs, such as CBN 700 Club. Her story has also been published in several articles, blogs, and books such as Unshackled and Free and LifeWay Magazine. As a radio talk-show host, internet Bible teacher, author, and encouraging speaker Patty has mentored and inspired millions with the hope of Jesus Christ and the power of His word.

Her books include:

Transformed by Desire: *A Journey of Awakening to Life and Love*

Finally Free: *Breaking the Bonds of Depression Without Drugs*

Experiencing Joy: *Strategies for Living a Joy Filled Life*

For more information about Patty Mason, her books or ministry, visit:

www.libertyinchristministries.com

54436323R00058

Made in the USA
Charleston, SC
01 April 2016